DUMP TRUCKS

Dan Osier

PowerKiDS
press.

New York

Published in 2014 by The Rosen Publishing Group, Inc.
29 East 21st Street, New York, NY 10010

First Edition

Editor: Amelie von Zumbusch
Book Design: Andrew Povolny
Photo Research: Katie Stryker

Photo Credits: Cover Ivaschenko Roman/Shutterstock.com; p. 5 Andrey N Bannov/Shutterstock.com; p. 7 Viktor1/Shutterstock.com; p. 9 Orange Line Media/Shutterstock.com; p. 11Goran Bogicevic/Shutterstock.com; p. 13 Bram van Broekhoven; p. 15 GTS Production/Shutterstock.com; p. 17 Wollertz/Shutterstock.com; p. 19 ndoeljindoel/Shutterstock.com; p. 21 Dragunov/Shutterstock.com; p. 23 Zacarias Pereira da Mata/Shutterstock.com.

Library of Congress Cataloging-in-Publication Data

Osier, Dan, author.
 Dump trucks / by Dan Osier. — First edition.
    pages cm. — (Construction site)
 Includes index.
 ISBN 978-1-4777-2862-8 (library) — ISBN 978-1-4777-2955-7 (pbk.) —
ISBN 978-1-4777-3032-4 (6-pack)
 1. Dump trucks—Juvenile literature. 2. Construction equipment—Juvenile literature. I. Title.
 TL230.O785 2014
 629.225—dc23
                               2013022428

Manufactured in the United States of America

CPSIA Compliance Information: Batch #W14PK3 For Further Information contact Rosen Publishing, New York, New York at 1-800-237-9932

Contents

Dump trucks carry big **loads**.
Then they dump them out.

The load goes in the truck bed.

A tarp may cover the bed. It keeps the load from spilling out.

The load must be balanced right. If it is not, the truck could tip over.

Dump trucks are called tipper lorries in Great Britain.

Off-highway dump trucks are the biggest kind. They are too big to go on roads!

You need a commercial driver's license to drive a dump truck.

Construction workers use dump trucks.

People in mines use them, too.
So do people on farms.

Have you ever seen a
dump truck?

WORDS TO KNOW

construction worker

dump truck

load

WEBSITES

Due to the changing nature of Internet links, PowerKids Press has developed an online list of websites related to the subject of this book. This site is updated regularly. Please use this link to access the list:
www.powerkidslinks.com/cs/dump/

INDEX